Original title:
Beneath the Coral Reefs

Copyright © 2025 Creative Arts Management OÜ
All rights reserved.

Author: Nora Sinclair
ISBN HARDBACK: 978-1-80587-258-0
ISBN PAPERBACK: 978-1-80587-728-8

Whispers of the Ocean Floor

The clams tell jokes, all quite absurd,
They giggle and shimmer, it's really unheard.
A starfish winks, with a sly little grin,
"Who knew sea life could be such a win!"

A crab with a hat struts by in a swirl,
"Check out my style, isn't it a thrill?"
The seaweed dances, a prankster's delight,
As fish roll their eyes, then take off in flight.

Secrets of Sunlit Waters

The trumpetfish toots, with a blast like a band,
While turtles rock shades, so cool and so grand.
A pufferfish puffs, then shrieks with a laugh,
"I'm the balloon king, now check out my half!"

The jellyfish jiggles, a wobbly sight,
While dolphins spin tales, with pure delight.
An octopus grins, ink clouds in the air,
"Hide and seek champ, you won't find me there!"

Dance of the Colorful Guardians

The angelfish prance in their shimmering suits,
While clownfish chuckle, in comedic pursuits.
They wiggle and giggle, all filled with glee,
"Who knew that the sea was a stage just for me?"

The sea urchin claims to be quite the star,
"Look at my spikes! They shine from afar!"
While parrotfish chat, with colors so bright,
They crack up the crowd with their comedic bites.

Hidden Kingdoms of the Deep

The seahorses race with a whimsical flair,
"Whose tails are the longest? It's a style affair!"
The grumpy old grouper just shuffles along,
Saying, "In this fish world, I still am the strong!"

A duo of shrimp, with teamwork so slick,
Outsmarting the predators, what a neat trick!
With bubbles and laughter, they frolic and play,
Underwater antics that brighten the day.

Wonders in the Aquatic Silence

In secret caves where fish do hide,
The clownfish plans his big joyride.
A turtle slurps on seaweed thick,
While octopus dances, oh so quick.

Shrimps throw parties with little flair,
While seahorses spin without a care.
The starfish plays a game of freeze,
As crabs conduct the symphony of seas.

A dolphin's joke, a surface splash,
Makes everyone giggle, oh what a clash!
With whispers of bubbles, all join in,
The laughter echoes, pure underwater din.

So here's to the antics, big and small,
In this watery realm, they amuse us all.
Who knew such fun could float about?
In the depths of blue, there's never a drought.

Shadows of the Playful Tide

The jellyfish waltzes, swaying slow,
While sea cucumbers steal the show.
A fish with glasses reads a book,
As the pouty pufferfish gives a look.

Crabs in tuxedos, oh what a sight,
Holding fancy balls each moonlit night.
Clams whisper secrets, sly and cheeky,
While turtles giggle, feeling quite freaky.

Starfish make wishes on ocean's tides,
While rascally dolphins take wild rides.
A mackerel dons a silly hat,
As plankton floats by, just like that!

So dive down deep, where laughter thrives,
With fishy fun under the tides.
In every bubble, a joyous cheer,
In the world below, there's nothing to fear.

Timeless Narratives of the Ocean's Embrace

The fish wear suits, quite dapper, in style,
They dance with grace, making us smile.
A crab plays chess, thinks he's so wise,
While seahorses giggle, oh what a surprise!

A starfish reads books, all out in the sand,
And octopuses juggle—such a sight, so grand.
But on Monday mornings, they just seem to yawn,
And the clowns of the sea say, 'Is it dawn?'

The Jewel Box of Nature's Depths

A treasure chest opens, with bubbles so bright,
Goldfish are holding a big dancing night.
They shimmy and shake, their scales all aglow,
While a clumsy old turtle steals all the show!

A dolphin in shades, looking suave and bold,
Sings karaoke, or so we are told.
The eels provide backup, with sparks and a twist,
It's the underwater party that can't be missed!

Life in the Liquid Labyrinth

Anemones whisper, their secrets so sly,
While clownfish are laughing, oh my, oh my!
The pufferfish blinks, in a puffed-up case,
'I've come to impress, just look at my face!'

A shrimp tells a joke, but no one will laugh,
Says, "It's all in the timing, have you heard my gaff?"
The language of bubbles they each understand,
In this maze of the sea, where silliness stands!

Echoing Songs of the Blue Abyss

With a splash and a dash, the mermaids all sing,
Their melodies echo, oh what joy they bring!
A whale joins the chorus, quite big and profound,
With a voice that can rattle the rocks on the ground.

The squid pipes up gently, with ink on his shirt,
While jellyfish dance like they've just come from dirt.
In the depths of the ocean, where laughter holds sway,
Every critter is jesting, come join in the play!

The Hidden Symphony of the Deep

Fish in tuxedos dance around,
With seaweed ties, they spin and bound.
Octopus plays the sax with glee,
Clownfish laugh, "Come swim with me!"

Shrimp hold a concert under the wave,
Shells are the stage where dancers behave.
Blowfish blow bubbles, quite the show,
Turtles tap dance, moving slow.

A crab with a hat takes the lead,
Jellyfish float, feeling freed.
Starfish clap, with arms out wide,
Underwater giggles, a joyful ride.

So come, dive deep to join the fun,
Where bubbles and laughter twirl as one.
In ocean's depths, there's music so sweet,
A hidden symphony to feel and greet.

Secrets of the Enchanted Sea

Seahorses whisper secrets galore,
Crabs gossip while hiding from shore.
Mermaids giggle, swishing their tails,
With funny tales of their fishy fails.

An eel throws a party, bright and grand,
With jellybeans falling like grains of sand.
Dolphins frolic and flip in delight,
While clams play cards late into the night.

A whale cracks jokes, deep as the ocean,
While small fish swim with fishy devotion.
Sea turtles tell tales of daring dives,
Chasing crabs in their colorful jives.

Such joyful chaos beneath the waves,
With laughter and antics, the ocean behaves.
Discover the whimsy within every reef,
Secrets of waters beyond all belief.

Enigmas of the Ocean Floor

Anemones wiggle, all in a twist,
As shy little fish play hide-and-seek missed.
Detective crabs scout for lost things,
While octopuses juggle with eight tiny rings.

Barnacles hope to win a race,
But sluggish clams just slow the pace.
Meet the grouper, dressed like a king,
With fishy friends, he loves to sing.

Mysterious treasures, each hold a tale,
A goldfish pirate who sails without fail.
The mystery deepens with every swirl,
As snails do a conga, giving a twirl.

Dive down below for a wild surprise,
Where laughter bubbles up to the skies.
The secrets concealed, oh what a sight,
Enigmas abound in the playful night.

The Hidden Gardens of Atlantis

In gardens where corals twist and twine,
Snails sip tea, saying, "Is this wine?"
Starfish frown with a puzzled look,
As sea cucumbers read a book.

Nemo's crew throws a garden bash,
With dancing sand dollars, oh what a splash!
Clams serve pasta on shining plates,
While jellyfish dance, no room for debates.

Each flower sways, in colors so bright,
Seahorses waltz, a comical sight.
Pufferfish chuckle, wearing a grin,
As the sea anemone spins in a spin.

So pluck the pizza from seaweed vines,
Join the hilarity where the sun shines.
The hidden gardens teem with delight,
A quirky world that's pure and light.

Guardians of the Undersea Canvas

In the depths where the fish wear tuxedos,
A crab tried to dance, but fell on his toes.
With seaweed wigs and bubbles galore,
The octopus laughed till he rolled on the floor.

Starfish thought they were great at charades,
But their arms got tangled in very strange ways.
A dolphin swam by with a cheeky grin,
Saying, "Who knew that sea life could be such a win?"

Chronicles of the Hidden Sanctuary

In a cave where the clams play hide and seek,
A fish wore a hat, quite the fashion geek.
The seahorses twirled, but got dizzy and spun,
They giggled and blushed, oh, what silly fun!

Jellyfish floated with grace and a sway,
Their tentacles twinkled, they danced through the fray.
While a clam tried to sing, but the sounds went awry,
The laughs echoed loudly, like bubbles that fly.

Murmurs of the Starry Sand

On the sandy floor, where the snails like to race,
A turtle took selfies, all smiles on his face.
With seagrass snacks, they enjoyed the sweet tease,
While a pufferfish puffed up, as big as he pleased.

A hermit crab switched shells, looking posh and prim,
Declared, "This new look really makes me quite slim!"
Meanwhile, the clownfish played jokes on their mates,
Sneaking up behind, then they disappeared – what great fates!

Dance of the Bioluminescent Spirits

At night the sea sparkles, a glow-stick parade,
With fish flashing lights like a disco charade.
A group of shy shrimps practiced tap on the sand,
While watching their pals throw a glow-stick band.

The lanternfish shimmered, they twirled and they spun,
With each little flicker, they shined like the sun.
Said a grouper, while giggling, "What a sight to behold!"
As creatures below sparkled in colors so bold.

The Realm of Underwater Wonders

In the ocean's colorful realm,
Fish wear ties, looking quite overwhelmed.
Surreal the seaweed dances with flair,
While crabs tap their feet with a snappy air.

A turtle on a skateboard speeds by,
Chasing a jellyfish who floats way high.
Starfish play poker on a sandy spree,
Cheering for clams sipping sweet iced tea.

Octopus chefs whisk in their little brown huts,
Cooking up meals with magical guts.
Seahorses race, oh what a sight,
Laughter bubbles up, day turns to night.

A World in Coral Embrace

In a cozy nook where the fish are bright,
Clownfish joke about their silly plight.
Anemone bouncers all stand so tall,
As they guide the newcomers, one and all.

A grouper with glasses reads the day's news,
While shrimps do the tango, refusing to snooze.
A dolphin hums tunes that tickle the gills,
And squid spread their ink like whimsical frills.

A crab tells tall tales of a giant whale,
As eels crack up over a fishy old tale.
The colorful corals keep giggling along,
In this underwater world, where everyone's strong.

Journey into the Aquatic Abyss

Dive into waters where giggles ignite,
Clownfish compete in a swim-off so tight.
A pufferfish snickers, its cheeks blown up wide,
As seahorses race, puffing with pride.

A shrimp style guru brings laughter with flair,
Teaching his buddies the latest cool hair.
Bubbles and gurgles, a comedian's sketch,
While a flatfish practices the art of a wretch.

Shy little octopi peek from their caves,
While a swordfish cries, "I'm a fish among waves!"
It's a splashy world where the humor is deep,
And down here the chuckles can make you lose sleep.

Where Fantasies Swim and Play

In a lagoon where the laughs overflow,
Dancing seashells put on quite the show.
Angelfish gossip with swanky old tales,
While sea cucumbers don't know how to sail.

A walrus cracks jokes, with a serious face,
As dolphins jump high, no slow or no pace.
Barnacles play marbles, under a big rock,
A mystical turtle checks his seashell clock.

A party of plankton swirls through the scene,
Completing their dance with a couple of beans.
It's a world where the bubbles tickle your feet,
A joyful parade, where all creatures meet.

The Allure of the Wave-kissed Kingdom

Fish in tuxedos, what a sight,
Dancing in bubbles, oh what delight!
A crab in a top hat, takes center stage,
While jellyfish juggle on a watery page.

Seahorses prance, with a flick and a flair,
Octopuses twirl without a single care,
Urchins grumble, they're not in the groove,
While mermaids giggle, with every sweet move.

Swaying Whispers of the Underworld

Starfish complain of their life on the floor,
Just lounging around, oh what a bore!
Anemones laugh, tickling with glee,
While clams play hide and seek, just you wait and see!

The turtles are gossiping, shells all aglow,
The dolphins are surfing, putting on a show,
While eels prank the fish with a wink and a smirk,
As the sea cucumbers just seem to lurk.

Whispers of the Aquatic Depths

A pufferfish puffed, said, "Look at me!"
A clownfish replied, "You're no one, just see!"
The anemones chuckled, their tentacles swayed,
As a sardine shoal hurried, oh what a parade!

Hermit crabs grumbled, stuck in their shells,
While snails plotted paths, with their slimy trails,
A parrotfish painted the reef with a smile,
In this underwater realm, all's quirky and wild.

Secrets of Submerged Gardens

Down in the depths, a garden grows bright,
With corals in colors that dazzle the sight,
A seaweed waltz puts the clownfish in trance,
While lobsters gossip, plotting their chance.

The starry night fish, with their shimmering glow,
Show off their moves, like a nighttime show!
But a grouchy old rockfish just wants to sleep,
Avoiding the laughter, in currents so deep.

Fantasies Under the Surface

In the sea where fish wear hats,
The starfish tap dance, oh what spats!
An octopus juggles shells with glee,
Laughing so hard, he drops a key.

Turtles sport shades while sunbathing,
Crabs play poker, their claws debating.
A seahorse twirls, quite the sight,
And all the coral chuckles in delight.

A dolphin wins the talent show,
Doing flips and splashes, quite the pro.
While a clownfish tells a silly joke,
And everyone giggles, even the bloke.

So dive in deep, and take a peek,
For underwater humor is quite unique.
With every wave, a chuckle waits,
In this kingdom where laughter creates.

Haven of the Reticent Creatures

There's a hermit crab who loves to hide,
Always shy, it's quite the ride.
He peeks from shells, avoiding the fuss,
While nearby shrimp just make a fuss.

A snail in pink just moves so slow,
Giving side-eye to the eel's show.
Fish gossip softly, keeping it light,
Whispers of dances in the moonlight.

A shy puffer fish blows up with fright,
Turns into a balloon, oh what a sight!
He floats away, with a squeaky cheer,
While all the seahorses gently leer.

In this nook, no loud debates,
Just quiet laughter and fishy mates.
With every wave, the giggles swell,
A secret world, where all is well.

The Symphony of Anemone Drifters

In pink and purple, they sway and dance,
   Anemones inviting with a chance.
   A fiddler crab plays tunes bizarre,
   While a jellyfish twirls, oh, so far.

With bubble notes that float through space,
   A clownfish joins in, keeps up the pace.
   The sea cucumbers clap along,
   To the rhythm of this cheery song.

The shrimp provide the beats with flair,
   While seahorses glide without a care.
   The octopus sneaks in with a grin,
Stealing the spotlight, let the fun begin!

Under the waves, an orchestra thrives,
   Where every creature cheerfully jives.
   With laughter echoing through the sea,
   The symphony plays, so wild and free.

Lost Legends of the Aquatic Realm

There was a crab who swam with flair,
Claimed he found treasure, but beware!
His legend spoke of golden pearls,
But it turned out to be just swirling swirls.

A fish who wore a tiny crown,
Was known for making the sea laugh out loud.
He told tall tales of monster size,
But it turned out they were just fish fries.

An old turtle shared underwater lore,
Of how to tango with a clam galore.
Yet when the moment finally came,
He slipped and tumbled, what a shame!

These myths float 'round like bubbles clear,
In the depths, we hold them dear.
With every swirl, a giggly tale,
In the ocean vast, where laughter prevails.

The Breath of the Sea

Fish in tuxedos dance with flair,
Crabs play poker, tossing their hair.
Bubble blunders, giggles galore,
Sea cucumbers roll, asking for more.

An octopus painting with eight tiny hands,
Slips and slides in silly bands.
Shark in a bowtie, too proud for the splash,
Snails on jet skis go whizzing past!

Treasures of laughter, shells full of cheer,
Turtles are juggling while munching their beer.
Seahorses tumble, roughhousing in style,
An underwater circus that brightens each mile.

Fantasies of the Forgotten Reef

A clam with a hat and a pearl necklace blings,
Tells tales of pirates and magical things.
Pufferfish giggle, blowing up wide,
As starfish take selfies, full of pride.

The conch shell gossip is really quite funny,
"Did you hear about Kevin? He lost all his money!"
Lobsters in shades breakdance on the sand,
With bubbles as microphones, oh isn't it grand?

The seaweed sways with an elegant flair,
While jellyfish twirl without a care.
Anemones crack jokes, tickling the fins,
In the carnival of life where the fun never ends.

Underwater Serenade

The clownfish laughs, 'What a sight to behold!
A sea turtle wearing pearls made of gold!'
A hermit crab sings, all gleeful and spry,
'Join me for karaoke, I'll give it a try!'

A school of fish starts a conga line,
While dolphins leap in rhythm and rhyme.
The sea is a symphony, wild and bright,
Where creatures unite from morning till night.

From planktonic waltzes to barnacle beats,
The sea urchins stomp with wiggly feats.
Coral formations sway with the tune,
As eels do the cha-cha beneath the full moon.

Riddles in the Tides

Why did the fish cross the ocean so wide?
To get to a party and dance with its pride!
A whale tells a riddle that breaks out in glee,
'What's big, blue, and floats? It's always just me!'

A crab with a monocle, quite the old sage,
Ponders the secrets of the underwater stage.
'What has a back but no body to hold?
It's a turtle's hard shell, so clever and bold!'

Seashells and treasures, where laughter is found,
In riddles and jests, all creatures abound.
Fantasy flows in each wave, a delight,
Joyous tales echo in the depths of the night.

Palette of the Deep

Colors swim and play, just like fish,
One's a clown, going "Hey! What's your wish?"
A lobster dances with bubbles galore,
While seahorses giggle, always wanting more.

An octopus juggling pearls with a grin,
Laughs at the starfish trying to spin.
The seaweed sways, doing a funky dance,
As the sea cucumbers just shyly glance.

A turtle practices yoga under the sun,
While parrotfish munch, thinking it's fun.
The crabs are holding a race, oh so quick,
With shells for helmets, they're quite the pick.

In this underwater carnival of cheer,
Everyone swims, and there's nothing to fear.
With tickles from currents, and laughter so free,
Oh, what a joyous, splishy-splashy spree!

Harmony in the Silent Waters

In the quiet depths, a jellyfish floats,
Waving its arms, like it knows all the notes.
A fish in a tuxedo, slick and so neat,
Cracks jokes with the shrimp, who can't handle the heat.

Anemones giggle as clowns pass them by,
"Stop tickling me!" they bubble, oh my!
While a grouper shows off its new fin bling,
With a wink and a nod, it's the underwater king.

Silly snails race on a slippery track,
With the dolphins cheering, they give them no slack.
In this tranquil realm, the laughter runs deep,
As bubbles and chuckles in harmony leap.

Whispers of laughter weave through the blue,
Every creature chuckles—yes, even the rue.
Under the waves, in a giggly ballet,
Life bubbles over, come join in the play!

Adventures in the Liquid Garden

In the garden below, where the fins take flight,
A crab with a cap starts a laugh-out-loud fight.
Starfish flipping like pancakes in the sun,
Their jokes are a treasure, oh, isn't this fun?

Bubble-blowers blowing the shapes of a moon,
While fish in top hats hold a late-night tune.
The driftwood's a stage, oh, don't miss the show,
As pufferfish puffs find their rhythm and flow.

A clam announces the start of the feast,
Where sea cucumbers give recipes at least.
"Add a pinch of sand, and a splash of the tide,
It's a recipe, my friends, that sea creatures abide!"

With every coral growing a brand-new smile,
Laughter echoes and spreads mile after mile.
In this liquid wonderland of joy and cheer,
The party keeps going, all year, oh dear!

Secrets Written on Shelled Pages

Amongst the shells lined up all in a row,
Whispering secrets that only fish know.
A crab reads a story, a twist and a turn,
With every flip page, new mischief to learn.

A clam plays the part of the wise old sage,
Sharing funny tales from a long, sandy age.
"Why did the turtle cross the ocean floor?"
"To get to the other tide, that's for sure!"

In the ink of the waves, all the laughter flows,
With dolphins in tutus striking their pose.
A snail on a scooter zooms past with flair,
Decked out in glitter, it flies through the air.

Secrets abound in this oceanic space,
With bubbles of giggles and smiles on each face.
So gather your treasures, let the fun begin,
In the depths where the laughter and secrets spin!

A Tapestry of Color and Wonder

A clownfish juggling with a sea sponge,
While sea turtles dance, oh how they plunge.
Bright parrotfish munch on coral snacks,
And octopuses play hide and attack!

Rainbow anemones wave with glee,
As starfish blunder, lost in the sea.
A shrimp in a top hat taps on the sand,
With laughter echoing through the vast land.

The seahorses prance in a silly parade,
Doing the cha-cha while never delayed.
A dolphin flips, and what a show,
All swim along, just enjoying the flow.

In this colorful world, what a delight,
Fish tell jokes in the deep of the night.
With bubbles of laughter, the bubbles rise,
Who knew the ocean held such surprise?

Treasures Buried in Swaying Gardens

A crab in a treasure chest, what a find,
With pearls that were stolen, oh so unrefined.
A grouper looks on, gives a wink, then a trot,
As he trips on a shell—what a silly plot!

The jellyfish sway like they're at a ball,
In dresses of silk, making quite the call.
An angel fish twirls with a flip of his tail,
While snails throw a party with a grand scale!

A conch shell giggles, it's tickled with foam,
As fishes rehearse, and they make it their home.
They grumble and bumble, but cheered by the crowd,
In their underwater realm—funny and loud!

What treasures are hidden, what joy can be found,
In gardens of laughter where jokes abound.
With a splash and a giggle, they frolic and flee,
These creatures in gardens, oh so carefree!

The Embrace of Currents and Colors

Currents entwine with a flick of their fins,
Fish spin and whirl—oh, where does it end?
A snapper throws confetti of shells in the breeze,
While a pufferfish blows up, just aim to please!

Glistening scales dance with a shimmer so bright,
As clownfish start cracking jokes left and right.
A stingray, quite lazy, lounges in the sun,
But a playful sea otter just won't let him be done!

The sea swirls with laughter, what a funny mess,
As eels do a conga, in sheer happiness.
A sea cucumber stumbles while holding a grin,
And everyone laughs, "Let the party begin!"

Caught in this whirlpool of joy and delight,
Bubbles of giggles float up to the light.
Currents may change, but one thing stays true,
The laughter that bubbles in oceans of blue.

Fauna's Ballet in Secret Grottos

In shadowy grottos where creatures take wing,
A flounder performs as the crab starts to sing.
Seahorses pirouette in their elegant way,
While schools of bright fish join the ballet!

A parrotfish shimmies, all decked out in style,
As the groupers cheer him with a wink and a smile.
Jellyfish drift by, in graceful, soft glow,
While the anemones giggle, "Go, go, go!"

The rhythm of currents is setting the stage,
As starfish clapped hands, oh, they're full of rage!
They stomp and they cheer, though they're stuck on the floor,
With no legs to dance, they shout, "We want more!"

With fins and with tails, they give it their all,
In this underwater theater, where all through the hall.
Laughter and music blend into the night,
In grottos of wonder, they twirl in delight!

The Sanctuary of Colorful Spirits

In a twisty dance, the fish all sway,
They giggle and wiggle, forget the day's play.
A pufferfish puffs, oh what a sight,
He tries to impress, but just gives a fright.

A crab wears a crown, made of seaweed too,
He struts on the sand, in his kingdom of blue.
With a wink and a nod, the seahorse prance,
As they all join in the underwater dance.

Murmurs of the Deep Sea

The clams are a-chatting, what secrets they share,
With a snap and a clap, they gossip with flair.
An octopus juggles shells, crazy and bright,
While the starfish just stares, glued to the sight.

A dolphin breaks in with a flip and a twist,
"Why don't you join me?" they all can't resist.
With bubbles of laughter, the sea comes alive,
It's a party down here, who needs to dive?

Colors Swirling Beneath the Waves

The anemones wave in a frilly ballet,
While clownfish make jokes in their own funny way.
A parrotfish raps, with a beat just so neat,
As the group crowds around for an impromptu treat.

A turtle ambles by, wearing a goofy grin,
He's searching for pizza, not on his skin!
With laughter and cheer, the ocean does hum,
In this vibrant bazaar, the fun's never done.

Tales from the Coral Sanctuary

A sleepy sea slug dreams of jellybean stars,
While the jellyfish twirl in their incandescent cars.
The fish share tall tales of a legendary catch,
Of a pirate who swapped, his treasure for scratch.

A lazy old turtle claims he's the fastest,
But the truth hits him hard, it's just quite the farce.
With a wink and a smile, the ocean spins tales,
Where humor's the currency, and joy never fails.

The Pulse of Marine Mysteries

In the sea where fish wear suits,
A clam once played a game of hoots.
He said, "My shell is quite a feat,"
As shrimp danced on with tiny feet.

A dolphin laughed, with a big splash,
"I'll never tell, I'm fast as a flash!"
The octopus waved his many arms,
"Catch me if you can, I bring the charms!"

The starfish grinned, laid back in delight,
"Most days, I just enjoy the night."
But when the seaweed starts to sway,
The underwater party's here to stay!

With bubbles popping, music plays loud,
A crab tried to dance, feeling quite proud.
But slipped on a jelly, what a sight!
The ocean chuckled through the night.

Lullabies of the Maritime Depths

Fish sing softly in shady beds,
Dreaming of past octopus threads.
"Why don't we float like bubbles do?"
Said the grouper with a fin so blue.

Anemones swayed to the ocean's beat,
Tickling the toes of a sleepy sea sheet.
"Let's nap on a reef, it's cozy and neat,"
Said the wise old turtle, taking a seat.

The seahorse sighed, "Wish I could sleep more,"
"Every time I close my eyes, I see the shore!"
A clownfish chuckled, "What's so wrong?
You could rock-a-bye in the coral throng."

In the dark where strange shapes creep,
Creatures snore softly, slumber deep.
But one little puffer just can't rest,
Every time he sneezes, he's the best!

Where Light Meets Liquid Shadows

When rays of sun meet the ocean's crowd,
The fish pose like models, feeling proud.
"Look, I'm a superstar!" a bright angelfish calls,
While clams hide in pearls, building their walls.

Clever little clownfish flip and dive,
Telling tall tales of how they thrive.
"A shark saved me once, but I took the bait,"
He giggles aloud, "what a twist of fate!"

A turtle chimed in, "I've seen better days,
Chasing lost flip-flops in a tidal maze."
But they all felt grand in their watery lair,
Beneath the giggles floating in the air.

As the waves roll in, they all frolic and play,
Each one a friend in this underwater ballet.
A sea cucumber took a bow with flair,
"Oh what a life, we're quite the rare!"

Treasures amid the Undulating Waves

A treasure map was lost in the tide,
"Oh no!" cried a crab, "where's my pride?"
With a laugh and a pirate hat, he set to roam,
Digging for treasures to call his home.

Fish took bets on where he would find,
A smoothie bar made of banana rind.
"Not gold or jewels, just a fruity treat,
That's the true prize—now isn't that neat?"

A seagull swooped and stole the map,
"Look at me!" it cawed, "I'm taking a nap!"
But while they all searched for gems and gold,
They found laughter—far richer than old.

In the end, it was shells and dreams,
And floating on waves with sweet humming streams.
So under the sea, they raised a cheer,
For treasures of friendship, ever so dear!

Undersea Kingdoms and Lost Legends

In schools of fish, they weave and play,
Flipping fins in a bright ballet.
With crusty crabs and silly snails,
They tell their tales with squeaky wails.

An octopus dons a top hat grand,
While turtles groan at the disco band.
A sunken ship drinks a bit too much,
And seashells giggle at every touch.

The seaweed sways like it's in a trance,
While clams are caught in a clumsy dance.
And every wave, a story spills,
Of frothy jokes and fishy thrills.

So dive right in, take a merry dip,
In this grand realm, don't let it slip!
For laughter reigns in this wavy land,
Where even the starfish form a band.

The Twilight Realm of Fishes

In twilight hues, the fishy jest,
Where guppies claim they're the best-dressed.
A pufferfish, with cheeks all round,
Tries to puff up, but still falls down.

The angelfish, with golden flair,
Bumps into shells with graceful air.
A clownfish waves its little fin,
"Why fit in when we can spin?"

With shrimp that dance on disco balls,
And jellyfish that bounce off walls.
Coral castles wobble and sway,
As fish paint selfies all day.

In laughter's tide, they happily float,
Each fish a swimmer, a giggling boat.
In this realm of bright twilight fun,
Where each day ends with a splashing pun.

The Dance of the Currents

The currents swirl, in playful jest,
As fishes spin like they're on a quest.
A seahorse twirls like a tiny knight,
In an ocean party, oh what a sight!

With eels that wriggle in toe-tapping glee,
And crabs that click with harmonies.
The marlins leap, and the squids do glide,
In a dance-off, who will decide?

Starfish stand as judges bold,
With a wink and a nod, their scores unfold.
Each bubble pops like a little cheer,
As laughter echoes through the sphere.

So join the jig of the ocean's beat,
With every wave, feel the rhythm's heat.
In this dance, where frolic meets,
Every fin flails, and joy repeats.

Refuge of the Resilient

In a buoyant world, the oddballs roam,
Where sea cucumbers make themselves home.
With a wink, a wink, and a wobbly shake,
Each creature thrives on the laughter they make.

The clownfish giggle in every nook,
While barnacles swap gossip with a hook.
A dolphin flips and cracks a joke,
As coral reefs warm up and poke.

With sea turtles dawdling in the sun,
They share their tales of the laughing run.
Anemones wiggle like they've lost their mind,
In this jolly refuge, comfort you'll find.

So take a plunge, let your worries drift,
In this amusing realm, the heart can lift.
For in this underwater spin,
Resilience wears a fishy grin.

The Symphony of Sea Creatures

In the giggle of fish, their fins do sway,
A crab with a hat dances night and day.
Octopus plays drums with his silly arms,
While seahorses twirl in their charming swarms.

The clownfish laughing, so brightly it glows,
Bubbles erupting from all of their throes.
A dolphin's quick wink, a mischievous tease,
Underwater antics that never cease.

Starfish playing tag on the sandy floor,
Hermit crabs rushing to settle the score.
Every wave a joke, the ocean's grand jest,
With guppies in tuxedos, oh what a fest!

Anemones wave like they've lost their sense,
In this raucous realm, it makes perfect sense.
Join the underwater fiesta and cheer,
For laughter and joy, under water, we steer.

Shadows of Forgotten Shipwrecks

Once there stood a pirate, with treasures so big,
His gold turned to coral, now it does jig.
A lobster claims the captain's lost chair,
While mermaids debate if it's time for a dare.

Jellyfish float like balloons in a breeze,
Telling tall tales as they bob with such ease.
Sea urchins gossiping like old time mates,
In a sunken abode filled with fishy debates.

The anchor now home to a family of snails,
Who laugh as the current tells old sailor tales.
While barnacles hum tunes on the rusty hull,
In this old watery grave that's never dull.

Crabs host a party, with a deck made of bones,
As seaweed sways in like it's chilling on phones.
Ghost ships are clapping to the beat of the tide,
With laughter and trips where the sea creatures hide.

The Ballet of the Nurtured Waves

Waves pirouetting, a dance of splashes,
Fish in ballet slippers, whoosh as they dashes.
Jellyfish twirl in a soft, gentle trance,
While sea turtles join in this watery dance.

The sea anemone sways to the beat,
As seahorses tango on their little feet.
Each ripple a step in a joyful parade,
Underwater glee that will never fade.

Starfish applaud with their five tiny hands,
Clams snapping shells like the best of bands.
Dolphins leap high, bowing with flair,
In this grand ballroom with naught but fresh air.

Algae twirls wildly like a disco ball,
While the ocean sings out a whimsical call.
With bubbles as confetti, the show will not cease,
In this buoyant ballet, we find such release.

Marine Mosaic: A Tapestry of Life

In patches of colors, the ocean does weave,
A mosaic so bright, it's hard to believe.
Fish with wild hairstyles swim here with zest,
While turtles in glasses claim they are the best.

Corals wearing hats made of sand and sun,
Invite all their pals for some silly fun.
With octopuses juggling bright beach balls,
And crabs throwing parties in fabulous halls.

Starfish play chess, their moves quite absurd,
While clowns of the sea shout, 'You've got my word!'
Underwater picnics with snacks that amaze,
Flipping for laughs in the sun's brilliant rays.

This wondrous world, where humor does thrive,
Keeps beating the odds, oh what a live jive!
In the colorful chaos, we find endless cheer,
A tapestry of laughter, where all gather near.

Currents of Forgotten Tales

A fish with a hat swam past a crab,
It tipped its brim, as if to nab.
The turtle chuckled at the sight,
'Is that hat for style, or a fishy fight?'

A seahorse danced on a floating leaf,
While octopuses played hide-and-sheaf.
The jellyfish winked with its glow,
'What shall we wear? A tutu or a fro?'

A clam decided to sing a tune,
With pearls that sparkled like the moon.
The pufferfish puffed, full of grace,
'This choir needs more space!'

Anemones giggled as they swayed,
'Is it our makeup that's gone astray?'
The world underwater spun with glee,
In this wacky, watery jamboree.

Echoes from the Silent Abyss

A whale tried to whisper, but it sneezed,
And sent bubbles flying, all quite pleased.
The dolphins laughed, oh what a mess,
'Sneezing underwater is quite the stress!'

A crab in a trench coat strutted along,
Singing catchy tunes, dancing a song.
'Watch me prance, for I have the moves!'
The fish clapped fins, 'Oh, what a groove!'

A starfish sat counting the shells on the floor,
Said, 'Can I breakdance? I just want more!'
With a spin and a flip, it fell on its face,
'Not sure this is my best showcase!'

The sea cucumber shrugged and slipped right past,
'Life is a party, make sure it's a blast!'
With laughter resounding from each tide,
The ocean's humor could not be denied.

Tides of Vibrant Dreams

A clownfish donned a bright yellow tie,
'Look at me, I'm classy, oh my, oh my!'
The angelfish giggled, 'A businessfish now?'
'You'll make quite the deal, take a bow!'

A hermit crab bragged of its new shell,
'It's the latest trend, can you tell?'
The seaweed swayed, caught in the thrill,
'Next season's style is a built-up hill!'

The parrotfish painted with coral hues,
Said, 'I'm the artist, what's in the news?'
The waters shimmered, sparkled with zest,
Each reef a canvas, they simply guessed.

The tides rolled in with sparkles so bright,
Casting dreams of delight in the moonlight.
'Let's dance like bubbles,' a group did declare,
With a splash and a giggle, it filled the air!

Enchanted Gardens of the Sea

A sea turtle found a flower so rare,
'I must show this treasure; it's beyond compare!'
The clownfish chuckled, 'Oh, that's quite bold!
Those petals are slippery, so be controlled!'

An octopus wore a necktie of kelp,
'With my gardening skills, I shall yelp!'
The coral giggled, 'You've made quite a scene,
An octo-gardener? It's a whole new routine!'

Starfish painted petals, quite like a pro,
While jellyfish floated, stealing the show.
'With each wave, our party will grow,
Just don't bring sea urchins, they steal the flow!'

In this garden of dreams, where fish twirl and play,
Every color and hue brings laughter each day.
The ocean, alive with giggles and glee,
Danced on forever, so wild and free.

Treasures Hidden in Green and Blue

In waters where the fish do dance,
A crab in trousers takes his chance.
He struts and poses, thinks he's bold,
While jellyfish are spinning tales of old.

A turtle lounges, quite the sight,
With goggles on, he feels just right.
He nods at shells, shows off his bling,
While seaweed whispers, 'Let's all sing!'

A clownfish grins with spots of orange,
Declares, 'I'm funny, not a foreign!'
His friends all chuckle, what a scene,
As they play peek-a-boo in sea's cuisine.

So come, dive deep into this spree,
Where silliness blooms beneath the sea.
Fishes giggle, and so do we,
In this underwater jubilee!

The Kaleidoscope of Reef Life

Bright fins flutter through the waves,
A parrotfish with giggle saves.
It chomps on coral, making snacks,
While seahorses wear tiny hats and slacks.

A grouper grins with all its might,
Cracking jokes at fishy night.
"Why don't oysters share their pearls?"
"Because they're selfish little whirls!"

The damselfish, a tiny sprite,
Tells stories that give all a fright.
With colors swirling in a dance,
They twirl and spin, each takes a chance.

In this carnival of fins and scales,
Every day brings silly tales.
So join the fun, splash and dive,
In this wacky world, we come alive!

Beneath the Shimmering Surface

A shrimp in shoes taps his tiny feet,
Boogieing to the coral beat.
While starfish fail to hit the floor,
Their limbs, like noodles, flop and soar.

A dolphin squeaks in rhymes so nifty,
"What's pink and goes hop? A jellyfish shifty!"
He flips and twirls in the brine,
While sea cucumbers grumble, "Oh, that's divine!"

The anemones wave, all in a row,
Throwing a party, don't be slow!
With squishy hugs and tickles galore,
They invite the fish to dance some more.

So laugh along in this funny place,
Where every creature wears a face.
In this sparkling sea of fun,
Every splash is a joke well done!

Marvels of the Ocean's Palette

In splashes of color, hyacinths bloom,
While lobsters strut, dispelling doom.
They color the sea with jokes and cheer,
Making octopuses giggle in sheer!

A boisterous blowfish puffs quite round,
Says, "Where's the seaweed? I'm feeling browned!"
His buddies chuckle, what a sight,
As they play tag in the fading light.

The angelfish flaunt their flashy fins,
Telling tall tales of their funny sins.
"Remember the time we painted a crab?
He was so mad, gave us the jab!"

So come on down, embrace the glee,
Where laughter bubbles in the sea.
With marbles of joy in every nook,
Join this funny fishy storybook!

Visions from the Abyssal Plains

Down in the depths, where the fish wear suits,
Crabs throw parties in their shell-shaped hoots.
An octopus juggles while the eels all cheer,
Singing fishy songs that only they can hear.

Jellyfish float, with a wobbly style,
Claiming to dance, though they've lost their guile.
"I'm a stunning star!" a flatfish will boast,
While the seahorses giggle, saying, "Stop, you're toast!"

Starfish adore to spread their arms wide,
Proclaiming to all, "We're the ocean's pride!"
They awkwardly pose on the sandy stage,
As the clownfish laugh, on every page.

In the deep, strange things do abound,
With laughter echoing in the playful sound.
So raise a fin high, let the good times roll,
In this underwater world, good humor's the goal!

Dancers in the Bubble Realm

Bubbles float by in a swirling cheer,
Turtles do the tango, with no one near.
Anemones sway in the gentle flow,
While the giggling plankton put on a show.

Shrimp in sequins, oh what a sight,
Twirl and twirl till they're dizzy with delight.
Clownfish crack jokes, while they steal the scene,
Pretending to be in a Broadway routine.

Pufferfish puff up for a grand ballet,
"This is how we dazzle," they shout, "let's play!"
Starfish spin in a fabulous flare,
As the seaweed waves like it's dancing air.

With currents that laugh and tides that tease,
The underwater bash puts all minds at ease.
So grab a sea partner and dance with glee,
In this bubble realm, joy is always free!

Reflections of Life in Coral Groves

In a garden of colors, the fish wear gowns,
Parrots of the sea, without any frowns.
Coral trees giggle, tickled by the tide,
Making room for the creatures who slip and glide.

A fish rode a wave, claiming, "Look at me!",
Only to trip on a bright anemone.
The corals burst out with laughter galore,
As the octopus hollered, "Hey, that's my door!"

Little shrimps race in their speedy parade,
While the sea cucumbers, just chill in the shade.
They wave lazy arms like they're sleepy posies,
Ignoring the fish with their charming do-si-do's.

Light dances softly through vibrant hues,
Creating a world full of whimsical views.
With laughter that bubbles like champagne in flows,
Life in the groves is a comedic prose!

The Ocean's Whispering Heart

With a secretive wink, the ocean will speak,
"Life here is fun, so come take a peek!"
Whales hum sweet tunes filled with jokes and glee,
While dolphins dive down in a bubbly spree.

Crabs sharing gossip, they click and they clack,
"Did you see that octopus? What a funny act!"
Coral critters chuckle, in a shimmering swirl,
"Oh look at that fish, he's lost in a whirl!"

Sharks in sunglasses, oh such a cool sight,
They strut and they flaunt, feeling oh-so-right.
In this whimsical world, hilarity flows,
As rhythm and laughter in harmony grows.

So let's dive deep to where the funny swarms,
With giggles and joy like oceanic storms.
A world of delight lies beneath every wave,
Where the ocean's heart promises fun to save!

The Play of Light on Marine Souls

In a dance of bubbles, fish wear a grin,
Clownfish cracking jokes, as the anemones spin.
A shrimp with red claws flaunts its style,
While turtles glide past, all slow, no rush, just a mile.

Bright rays tickle scales, a shimmering show,
Octopus winks, in disguise aeons ago.
Seahorses chuckle, in their twisty wraps,
Their tiny jokes echo like underwater claps.

The ocean's a stage, with drama untold,
Where eels play peek-a-boo, so daring, so bold.
Jellyfish jive, with neon delight,
While the sun smiles down, faced with pure light.

Each wave is a giggle, each splash is sheer fun,
In this world of sea creatures, the laughter's just begun.
With fins and a flare, they twist and they twirl,
In a watery realm, under laughter's swirl.

An Odyssey Through Living Waters

It's a fin-tastic voyage, with friends in the tide,
Where a crab tells tall tales with great ocean pride.
A dolphin's quick quips bring a wave of delight,
While squids squirt ink, a comedic fright!

Snails racing snappily, though they're not quite fast,
Bumping into rocks, what a funny contrast!
Starfish practice yoga, all spread out on a rock,
While a sea cucumber's busy with its tick-tock.

The fish sing a tune, with bubbles as notes,
They harmonize sweetly, like little boat mopes.
With seaweed swinging, as if it can dance,
The ocean's a party, come join in the chance!

Adventures abound, in the kelp's gentle sway,
With crabs in tuxedos, they dance night and day.
The laughter is endless, as explorers unite,
In this funny aquatic world, quite the sight!

Secrets of the Silent Depths

In the hush of the blue, where secrets reside,
A fish wears a mask, but it's not trying to hide.
With wise old turtles, who nod and just grin,
They chuckle at bubbles, and the chaos within.

Clams keeping gossip, with shells clamped so tight,
Whispers of octopi and their marvelous plight.
A pufferfish snickers, 'I'm spiky, beware!'
While angelfish giggle, with glittery flair.

The sea stars keep watch, all twinkly and bright,
Sharing tales of lost ships that drift out of sight.
Anemones laugh, with tentacles loose,
Telling shrimp to chill, "Come here for a moose!"

In this silent ballet, there's humor galore,
With jests of the depths, who could ask for more?
As bubbles tickle laughter along the sea floor,
The secrets unfold, in waves of rapport.

Glide of the Gentle Current

In currents that giggle, and swirl in delight,
The fish cruise along, all graceful in flight.
A lazy old shark, with a toothy big grin,
Mumbles, "I'm friendly, come on, let's swim!"

The sea otters tumble, spinning round with glee,
While clowns in the coral are tickling a spree.
Whale songs echo with a humorous twist,
As they sing of adventures, that cannot be missed.

With bubbles in tow, seahorses parade,
While the crabs keep on prancing, they simply won't fade.

Hooray for the currents, that carry us through,
With laughter in pockets, in this dreamlike blue.

The frolicsome flow, is a delightful chase,
With smiles infinite in this underwater space.
From fishy conspiracies to sea fans that sway,
The glide of this current brings laughter our way.

Echoes Among the Anemones

A clownfish juggles seaweed,
With a giggle and a grin,
He makes a great comedian,
In the dance of ocean's din.

An octopus with eight arms wide,
Tries to pickle a lost shoe,
But the crabs all laugh and slide,
As they offer a fishy stew.

Starfish wear sunglasses bright,
As they soak up salty rays,
They gossip about the night,
Under the moon's playful gaze.

A turtle tells a tall tale,
Of a wave that turned to bread,
And all the fish sail and sail,
While dreaming of a feast ahead.

The Colorful Kingdom Below

A parrotfish paints the scene,
With colors loud and bright,
He gives the coral a sheen,
While the seahorses take flight.

A pufferfish who loves to puff,
Balloons into a sight,
When asked if he's had enough,
He giggles and takes a bite.

Shrimps tap dance on the sand,
With tiny toes so neat,
They form a little band,
For all the sand dollars to seat.

The jellyfish float with flair,
In an ever-swaying show,
Beneath the sun's warm stare,
They wave and giggle, just so!

Mysterious Currents and Vibrant Life

A grouper with a fine mustache,
Claims he's the ocean's king,
While sardines dash in a flash,
Singing songs and doing their thing.

The sea urchins have a plan,
To throw a pointy ball,
But when it rolls, oh what a span,
They all laugh and start to sprawl.

A dolphin dons a hat too big,
And tries to dive so sleek,
But he tumbles with a gig,
And lands with a splashy squeak.

Anemones wave their hands,
In a rhythmic, snappy dance,
They tickle passing fishy bands,
Who can't help but join the prance.

Dreams in the Ocean Blue

A fish dreams of a golden throne,
Crafted from seaweed strands,
He snoozes on a coral stone,
While plotting grand piano lands.

A lobster plays the tambourine,
With claws that clap and sway,
While jellyfish join in between,
In a sticky, sweet ballet.

The sea cucumbers take a break,
And join in for a jest,
They try to bounce, oh what a quake,
And chuckle at their best.

With all the sea critters bold,
The laughter flows like wine,
In the depths, stories unfold,
Where humor and friendship entwine.

Tide Pools of Enchantment

In a tide pool, fish play hide and seek,
A crab waves hello with a quirky beak.
Starfish twirl in a slow-motion dance,
While seaweed giggles, giving all a chance.

The sea snail moves at a snail's pace,
In this magical, slippery space.
A shrimp does the cha-cha, without any fear,
While seagulls watch, wishing they had beer.

The bottle caps tumble, a treasure scoffed,
As hermit crabs claim homes never lost.
Anemones blush with pride and glee,
In the frothy waves of a salty spree.

As the tide retreats, the laughter flows,
In the dance of creatures nobody knows.
With a wink and a wave, the tide pools sigh,
For tomorrow's show, they'll let it all fly!

Sunlight Dancing on Ocean Floors

Sunlight twinkles like diamonds on fins,
Fish flip and flop, doing goofy grins.
Seahorses giggle, riding the current,
A jellyfish bobs, looking quite fervent.

An octopus twirls in a disco move,
While clams clap along, trying to groove.
The floor's a stage, for all to partake,
Crabs form a band, making waves that shake.

A dolphin dives down, trying to steal,
The spotlight with flips, what a big deal!
The sunbeams shimmer, laughter cascades,
As creatures join in this silly charade.

With bubbles and splashes, they reach for the sky,
In this underwater party, oh my oh my!
The laughter and fun fill the watery space,
While sunlight keeps dancing, lighting the place.

Castles Made of Coral

A castle of coral, bright pink and blue,
Where fish throw a party, just for the crew.
The gates are sea urchins, spiky and round,
While seahorses charge in with a giggly sound.

The party's in full swing, balloons made of kelp,
With dancing crabs moving, oh what a help!
Starfish serve snacks, all salty and sweet,
As turtles breakdance on their flippers and feet.

The mermaids show up, bringing laughter and cheer,
With bubbles for drinks, they toast with a beer.
A clam plays the piano, it's quite the surprise,
As fishes dive in for a musical rise.

They boogie till dusk in this colorful land,
With coral confetti drifting like sand.
In castles of coral, where fun never ends,
The ocean's the place where laughter transcends!

Journey Through a Marine Wonderland

Join the parade where the sea critters roam,
A wiggly eel leads the way back home.
The pompoms are jellyfish, bouncing with style,
While fish form a conga, lasting a while.

Turtles race by in slow-motion bliss,
Trying to catch the odd sea cucumber kiss.
A dolphin yells out, "Let's jump and swim!"
And with every cheer, the lights start to dim.

The clowns of the ocean, the painted gobies,
Tell jokes to the group, all laughing like hobies.
With sea turtles rolling and crabs in a whirl,
Adventure is waiting, so give it a twirl!

A seaweed forest, a maze to explore,
With secret clues left on the sandy floor.
In this marine wonderland, fun's the decree,
Where everyone swims with hilarious glee!

www.ingramcontent.com/pod-product-compliance
Lightning Source LLC
Chambersburg PA
CBHW060143230426
43661CB00003B/545